Hold That Thought

Hold That Thought

The Reality Is Closer
Than You Think

Saundra Hagans

Kingdom Living Publishing
Accokeek, MD

Hold That Thought
© 2019 by Saundra Hagans

Cover title concept by Mogul Focus, LLC (www.mogulfocus.com) Cover layout anddesign by TLH Designs, Chicago, IL (www.lovetl-hayden.com)

Published by:

Kingdom Living Publishing
P.O. Box 660
Accokeek, MD 20607

Published in the United States of America.

ISBN 978-0-9968089-4-1

ISBN 978-0-9968089-5-8 (eBook)

Dedication

This book is dedicated to my daughter Sharae M. Ingram, my granddaughter Najia N. Hall, and my grandson Joshua Diyalukila. The three of you have grown by quantum leaps. So proud of you.

Contents

Chapter 1

Hold That Thought

Then God said, "Let Us make man in Our image, according to Our likeness; let them have dominion over the fish of the sea, over the birds of the air, and over the cattle, over all the earth and over every creeping thing that creeps on the earth." So God created man in His own image; in the image of God He created him; male and female He created them. Then God blessed them, and God said to them, "Be fruitful and multiply; fill the earth and subdue it; have dominion over the fish of the sea, and over the birds of the air, and over every living thing that moves on the earth" (Genesis 1:26-28).

After God created Adam and Eve, the first thing He did was give them authority over the earth and thoughts to hold. *As a man thinks, so is he.* God told them what they could accomplish; He spoke blessings over Adam and Eve. Those blessings enabled them to be progressive in their thoughts and actions. The progressive thoughts and actions resulted in them having the ability to carry vision, dream dreams, and be productive. Everything was subject to the man and to man's authority.

Have you ever wondered what happened to their thoughts when everything one could ever hope to have was at their disposal? Just think about their environment: The earth was yielding good fruits and vegetables; they had the best gold, pearls, onyx stones, wonderful rivers of water, and so on. They had all the "bling" one could ever want. Everything on the earth was subject to them. They had a great life, just spending time with God and with each other.

What were you thinking? Wouldn't you like to pose that question to Adam and Eve?

And out of the ground the Lord God made every tree grow that is pleasant to the sight and good for food. The tree of life was also in the midst of the garden, and the tree of knowledge of good and evil (Genesis 2:9).

And the Lord God commanded the man, saying, You may freely eat of every tree of the garden; but of the tree of the knowledge of good and evil and blessing and calamity you shall not eat, for in the day that you eat of it you shall surely die (Genesis 2:16-17 AMPC).

Here we find God giving them a thought to hold onto that involved choices—to obey or not to obey. Our Father does not want us to be puppets, nor does He want us to have the feeling of being controlled; He wants us to obey Him, to believe He knows what is best for us as well as have faith in the fact that His thoughts toward us are good thoughts.

Frank Sinatra's song titled "*I Did It My Way*" is one that most of us can attest to. There have been times in my own life when I wished God would have intervened, by giving me visions of stop signs, red lights with warnings blasting all around me. However, He gave us something better than siren sounds. He gave us Holy Spirit. Holy Spirit will speak to us very gently while attempting to steer us away from the wrong tracks but He will not strong arm us. He wants us to love Him with all our heart, with all our soul, mind, and strength. So, locked up in the tree of life were things precious and beautiful, such as the abundant life, everlasting life on earth, happiness, strength, freedom from bondage, sickness, evil thoughts, continuous refreshing and renewal, wisdom, revelation, and knowledge. All of this was theirs for the taking. The tree of life was intended to bring continuous development to their spirit man whereas the tree of knowledge of good and evil brought about the development of their soul and slow death to the spirit.

Now the serpent was more cunning than any beast of the field which the Lord God had made. And he said unto the woman, "Has God indeed said, 'You shall not eat of every tree of the garden'?" (Genesis 3:1). Satan knew that once the spirit was weakened and eventually depleted, man would become independent and self-serving and eventually ease God out. He knew that man would become prideful and inevitably would be a man that is led by his soul resulting in Satan having access to control the personality of man. Satan hates God, and therefore he hates and detests us because we are the children of God, created in His image and likeness. He wants to devour you without mercy. He likes to traffic your mind with evil thoughts and much confusion. If the devil can cause you to question the Word of God, the voice of God or His leading, or if he can introduce an ounce of doubt and cause you to wonder, Did God say that, or did He mean to say something else? He can gain access to your thinking and begin to build strongholds in your mind.

The devil's intent is to blind your mind (2 Corinthians 4:4). The word "blind" here means one who is unable to discern or judge; to hide from sight, to harden one's heart, render stupid or callous. We perish for lack of knowledge, and it is the devil's greatest desire for us to live in total ignorance to the truth of God's Word by placing blinders on your heart and mind. This is why Peter says for you and me to *"gird up the loins of your mind, be sober, and be mentally alert."* Your defeat or victory begins with your thoughts.

> *And the woman said unto the serpent, we may eat of the fruit of the trees of the garden. But of the tree which is in the midst of the garden, God hath said ye shall not eat of it, neither shall ye touch it, lest ye die* (Genesis 3:2-3 KJV).

It is obvious that Eve had been told by her husband what the Lord said. I assume Adam explained the importance of being obedient to God and perhaps they even tried to comprehend the possibility of dying, but it was inconceivable since abundant life was freely flowing in their midst.

Beware of Satan's demonic influence. Anytime he can convince one-third of the angels residing in heaven to forsake all and follow Him, you know he can as my daughter says "sell ice to an Eskimo." Eve was under this demonic influence, and it caused her curiosity to be aroused. Do you recall the times when perhaps your parents forbid you to do something, and as soon as they turned their backs, you did exactly what they told you not to do? Adam and Eve were not made as robots; therefore, they were able to make decisions according to their will. Just think, if you were told you could have everything around you except one big, beautiful, and harmless looking thing, would not your interest be peaked? Rising every morning, passing by the one beautiful and harmless looking thing you cannot have and not fully comprehending why you have been deprived of something that seems so harmless, would not your interest be peaked? Perhaps you would wonder if I have ninety-nine percent, why cannot I have the other one percent. Moving away from the thoughts of God can start with the first drink, the first drug "hit," a one-night stand, the first visit to the club or any of the many indiscretions you and I may have or still are engaged in. The enemy of our soul is among other things, an opportunist, he crouches at the door of our hearts waiting for a place of entry. We are to give no place to the enemy, for once his foot has been wedged in the open door of opportunity, the spiritual warfare begins.

Then the serpent said to the woman, "You will not surely die. For God knows that in the day you eat of it your eyes will be opened, and you will be like God, knowing good and evil" (Genesis 3:4-5).

Isn't it interesting that Eve knew what the Lord said, but despite her knowledge of God's Word, the devil boldly indicated that God was lying and that He obviously wanted to hide something much more spectacular than what they had experienced to that point and what God had already freely given them? Do not underestimate Satan!!! As I stated earlier, and this bears repeating, he was in the very presence of God and all His glory, yet he was able to influence one-third of the angels to follow him into rebellion. The dictionary defines influence as "corrupt interference with authority for personal gain." Satan has a strong spirit of influence, and as he used influence in heaven, here again, his demonic influence is used in the garden.

The devil is on a mission to introduce doubt and confusion; he knows that doubt will cause one to question God's motives and bring about cloudy and misguided thoughts. Think about it; all Adam and Eve knew was good. They were wealthy, healthy, pioneers, dominion takers, and intelligent. They were familiar with the agape love with God and with unashamed love for each other. They had nothing to fear because they were unfamiliar with fear. There was nothing in existence in the garden of Eden to bring them into any type of bondage. They could look at one another lovingly and only see the glory of God; they were naked without shame. But the enemy said wait. You do not know evil; you do not know pain and sickness; you do not know hate and unforgiveness; you do not know how to function without God's interference.

Apparently, evil was not a word that Eve was familiar with. A few definitions of the Hebrew meaning of the word evil are wicked evil thoughts, unpleasant, giving pain or causing unhappiness.

The devil was saying to Eve, go ahead, touch it, eat from it, and the moment you do, your body will begin decaying; your thoughts toward your husband will be one of suspicion, jealousy, and anger; your children will be born into this world at a disadvantage; a generational curse will be your portion. Your relationship with God will be affected, and instead of walking and talking with Him, shame will cause you to run and hide. He knew the moment they ate from the tree, their destiny would be altered, and life as they knew it would never be the same. The enemy of their soul knew that if they failed to hold on to that thought received during their initial conversation with God, that he could gain place. *If you do what is right, will you not be accepted? But if you do not do what is right, sin is crouching at your door; it desires to have you, but you must rule over it* (Genesis 4:7 NIV).

For though we walk in the flesh we do not war after the flesh. For the weapons of our warfare are not carnal, but mighty through God to the pulling down of strongholds. Casting down (lower and demolish) imaginations (reasoning, empty assumption, and mind creations) and every high thing that exalts itself against the knowledge of God and bring into captivity (prison of war) every thought (perception or device) to the obedience (attentive hearkening, submission) of Christ (2 Corinthians 10:3-5).

When the enemy decides he's going to take his best shot at you and he begins to take final steps toward causing your thoughts to line up with his thoughts, he releases what the Bible calls fiery darts with the intent of destroying with fire every truth you know. At the same time, he makes it difficult for the entrance of God's Word to give light to the darkness he has created in your soul. Also, the fiery darts' intent is to render you weak, passive, and helpless. The strongholds are built in your mind by him because he wants to dominate your personality.

Ephesians 6:16 (AMPC) says, *"Lift up over all the [covering] shield of faith, upon which you can quench all the flaming missiles of the wicked [one]."* When you decide that enough is enough, then you will have joined the forces of the violent ones who take control of their mind by force; you make the decision to be alert and sharp in your thinking. This is the time for those rivers of living waters to begin to flow from your belly. You are not to take the enemies suggestions lightly, nor are to you entertain the thoughts he fires at you, but you must bring every demonic thought down with God's truth. The Word of God is like a hammer and fire. You must choose to smash and burn the fiery darts that are aimed at your mind. When the apostle Paul referred to the word imaginations, he was talking about hostile intentions toward the gospel of Christ. This is why there has to be a casting down. Once they are down, put your feet on those toxic thoughts, trampling and reigning over them. Additionally, you have to take this fight to another level by discerning the ways of God; for the devil will present himself to you as an angel of light and if you are not astute enough to discern the things of the spirit, you will be fooled into thinking that what you just heard was a "God thought."

Arrest thoughts that are toxic and irritating to your spirit. Our Father is a God of peace. When He speaks to your spirit, you will experience His peace. If you find yourself wrestling with the thoughts and becoming confused and uneasy, most likely, God was not speaking to you, so do not entertain the thoughts. The Scripture says to cast down everything that exalts itself against the knowledge of God. The word knowledge here means to know experientially; in other words, there must be a working knowledge of the thoughts of God. Therefore, relationship and intimacy with the Lord are essential: *He who dwells in the secret place of the Most High shall remain stable and fixed under the shadow of the Almighty (whose power no foe can withstand)* (Psalm 91:1 AMP). Making the secret place the place where you dwell habitually will assure soundness of mind.

The Lord says, *"My sheep know My voice."* Just as we know the distinctiveness of our parents' voices, the same should be true when it comes to hearing the voice of our heavenly Father. As we habitually dwell in that secret place and become more and more familiar with His ways and His voice, the enemy will not be able to intrude into our thoughts so easily. Our spiritual alarms will go off instantly to warn us that there is a mental intrusion. You must evict the squatter(s). They are illegally occupying your space; they broke in and took up residence without legal rights. Put them out!!! Cast them down!!! Take legal action; do not give evil/demonic thoughts a stay; execute them immediately; pull the switch; bury the toxic thoughts; cast them down and keep them down.

Ephesians 2:6 (AMPC) states, *"And He raised us up together with Him and made us sit down together (giving us joint seating with Him) in the heavenly sphere (by virtue of our being) in Christ Jesus (the Messiah, the Anointed One)."* The Lord has given us a high position in that He has given us an exalted seat in heavenly places. This must be more to you than a positional seat; it must become the seat you have sat in and have experienced. In other words, the Lord Jesus Christ as a result of the finished work on the cross has equipped you with delegated authority. You have the armor of God, power from on high, spiritual gifts, the infilling of Holy Spirit and angels that are encamped around you to name a few things. Now you must rise to the occasion with the ammunition that has been made available to you and protect your thoughts at all cost.

Chapter 2

Take No Thought

Therefore, I say unto you, take no thought for your life, what ye shall eat or what ye shall drink; nor yet for your body, what ye shall put on. Is not the life more than meat, and the body than raiment? Behold the fowls of the air: for they sow not, neither do they reap, nor gather into barns; yet your heavenly Father feedeth them. Are ye not much better than they? (Matthew 6:25-26 KJV).

Giving thought to tomorrow robs you of the joy you can experience today. This Scripture had special meaning to me some years ago. I was going through what seemed to be one of the worse times of my life. My short-lived marriage had just ended, and I had to leave town to avoid my ex-husband's threat of death being fulfilled. I left my child behind, quit my job, and moved to a state many miles away from my hometown. It seemed like everything I touched at that time was turning against me. I went from job to job, not because I did not want to work but because the employers were experiencing federally funded cuts. I felt like I was at my wits end living in a strange city without family and friends to rely on. It was during this time that I found Matthew 6:25-26, and I read it every day. Note, I said I found the Scripture because during that time I very rarely read the Bible. As a matter of fact, I did not own a Bible; the one I was reading was received as a giveaway from a church I had visited. As I continued to read the word, I noticed changes were taking place in my circumstances. Please understand, I was not spiritually mature at that time, so I did not have the presence of mind to give God all the credit for the changes that were taking place. Reading the Bible came as a last-ditch effort on my part because I thought I was losing my mind.

God is so amazing, awesome, and kind. I was doing worldly things and not totally acknowledging Him (the Lord was acknowledged by me only during those times when I was not able to handle things on my own). Yet, He still released His goodness towards me and begin to bless me in my place of hurt, pain, fear, and lack. I was in a place physically and mentally where I had never been before. I was a very independent person and was always able to provide for myself, but now I had found myself alone with no one to call on but Jesus. He showed up and began to show me favor, and He caused men to show me favor as well. The awesome thing about the situation back then was that He did not give me what I deserved based on my sinful lifestyle. He dealt with me according to where I was going not where I was. Since then, the question I have had to ask myself during those times of more tests, trials, and affliction is "If He brought you out back then when you didn't know Him, what do you think He will do on my behalf now that I am born again and serving Him with my whole heart."

So, the Lord says to us in Matthew 6:25, stop worrying, stop fretting and sweating the small stuff. Your life is valuable to Me; you are precious in My sight. My Son has paid the ultimate price for you to be free from poverty and lack. I sent Him "on purpose" so that you could enjoy the highest and best life, the life that over and above exceeds your expectation: *I am come that they might have life, and that they might have it more abundantly* (John 10:10). So, why are you giving thought to small insignificant things like bills, groceries, rent, mortgage, etc.? When in fact the birds that we are told to consider are always unemployed. All they do is hang out in trees, on top of wires, and atop peoples' homes; they fly around, taking in the breeze and yet not one has fallen from a tree because he was starving. God continues to supply their needs daily. And He is doing the exact same thing for you because He promised that He will never leave you nor forsake you.

The next verse goes on to say *"Are ye not much better than they?* The amplified version says, *"Are ye not worth much more than they?"* Have you considered your worth? Perhaps if you knew what value you hold in the kingdom of God, you would not dare think that your heavenly Father would allow you to experience lack or want; after all, you are His son and daughter. As Philippians 2:5 says, *"Let this mind be in you, which was also in Christ Jesus."*

As you read the Word of God, challenge yourself. Start taking mental photos of yourself; begin to imagine yourself being blessed mentally sharp and brilliant. See yourself as one who is goal oriented, healed, always being an overcomer, and a great warrior with much confidence. With the mind of Christ, see yourself as a portrait of success, with the blemishes of failure and the wrinkles of weakness having been retouched until you see the perfect picture.

Psalm 27:13 says, *"I had fainted unless I had believed to see the goodness of the Lord in the land of the living."* Yes, there are times when you may feel completely overwhelmed by your circumstances and situations. Yes, there are times when you may say to yourself, "I give up, forget it." Trust me when I say life can throw some curves at you and that will make you wonder as the Israelites wondered if God can, in fact, provide a table in the wilderness. There may be times when you are tempted to feel depressed and oppressed because you do not see a way out. You do not see the light at the end of the tunnel. You have tried this, and you have tried that; you decreed, and you declared; you fasted and prayed. You attended Sunday worship, midweek services, as well as attended every service the church offered, and you are still wondering where God is. Or, have you ever watched the saints shout and dance during worship services while you sat there wanting to say to them, "What are you so happy about? Don't you see my pain, my hurt, and shame? Aren't you discerning I'm losing it?" And oh boy, do not let someone stand up and give a testimony about their new car or home and you are using public transportation and can hardly pay your rent. Does it make you feel like you have been overlooked by heaven? Moreover, the enemy will begin to tap into your negative emotions. He will magnify your situation, and if you are not careful, he will tell you God is not concerned about you. He will tempt you to long for the things of the world to pacify your temporary state. Daniel said, *"They that know their God will be strong and do exploits."* (See Daniel 11:32.)

Take time to understand how the Lord moves in your life, and what He requires of you during your various seasons of growth and maturity. Times of testing is the opportune time to develop a deeper relationship with the Lord. By deepening your relationship, you will come to the place where like James, you will *count it all joy when you fall into divers temptations* (see James 1:2-4). As patience has her perfect work in you, you will find yourself giving thanks and praise for what the Lord is about to do. Spending quality time with Him will cause you to arrive at a place in your thought life where you are fully persuaded that His thoughts toward you are not evil, but good and that the entire journey was put in motion to bring you to your expected end. (See Jeremiah 29:11.)

Chapter 3

Transformation by Mind Renewal

"For My thoughts are not your thoughts, nor are your ways My ways," says the Lord. "For as the heavens are higher than the earth, so are My ways higher than your ways, and my thoughts than your thoughts" (Isaiah 55:8-9).

As I sat at my computer, my mind wandered off to those many times when I relied on my own intellect—oops, I mean foolishness in making decisions concerning my life. I can honestly tell you that I have taken some major detours that always led to either destruction, body trauma, a broken heart, or a demolition derby type situation. My thoughts and deeds were clouded with things like pride, self-determination, and the need to survive in a world that I had basically created or that had been created via generational curses. My thinking did not begin to change until after I was spirit filled. It was then that I understood that my steps are ordered by the Lord, not Saundra L. Hagans. After being filled by the Spirit of God, my hunger and thirst for the Word of God, the wisdom and revelation of God, were stirred. I begin to experience wisdom for God which enabled me to realize Jesus wanted to be the Lord over my ways and thoughts. The more I yielded to the Word of God and became more familiar with God's way of thinking, the more I was positioned to be in His will for my life. It was a relief to know I did not have to give thought to tomorrow, that I do not have to plan for my future alone, and that I have access to the mind of Christ and do hold the thoughts, feelings, and purposes of His heart. I can now set goals and objectives based on His will for my life and have confidence in knowing that it is His idea, His plan, and His will for my life.

Romans 12:2 tells us that we are not to be impressed or influenced by the world's ways of thinking and doing, but we are to undergo a deep inner change, a metamorphosis ("a change of physical form, structure, or substance especially by supernatural means") (Merriam-Webster Dictionary). This transformation takes place from within and causes one to turn from the old and embrace the new. The places you used to go are no longer appealing; the people who at one time you thought you could not do without suddenly are no longer appealing to you. With this transformation your mind refocuses, and your thoughts are gradually on the things above resulting in offensive thoughts having difficulty entering your mind. You gradually become skilled in casting the imaginations down and putting the fiery flames out. Your thoughts will begin to continually transcend and align themselves with divine thoughts that are influenced by the kingdom of God. All of this gives you the ability to walk in kingdom dominion and power with the authority that is rightfully yours.

Your mind must be transformed and renewed daily to fully comprehend what God wants to do in each season of your life, and for you to be in agreement with His plan for your life. Third John 2 says, *"Beloved, I wish above all things that thou mayest prosper and be in health, even as thy soul prospers."* The Greek word for soul is psoo-khay. This word refers to the mind of an individual. Everything you accomplish in the spirit realm depends on the prosperity of the mind: *But we have the mind of Christ (the Messiah) and do hold the thoughts (feelings and purposes of His heart)* (1 Corinthians 2:16 AMPC). Here we see that available to the body of Christ are His supernatural thoughts, an ability that enables us to think like He thinks without leaning to our own understanding.

Our Lord Jesus Christ has raised us up and given us a portion of His kingdom's power. He has given us the spiritual authority and ability to be more than conquerors, to be overcomers, and to live a life of complete victory. He has given us a seat in heavenly places where there are no hindrances or delays to His will being completely fulfilled. We are structured to function both in the earth realm and the heavenly realm. Our body needs its earth suit to be relational to the earth; the purpose of our spirit man is to enable us to relate to the spirit realm.

Chapter 4

You Were Created to Glorify God

Even every one that is called by my name: for I have created (chosen/selected) him for My glory (splendor and honor), I have formed him (as a potter to clay fashioned and framed and given him purpose); yea I have made him (appointed, brought forth and maintained) (Isaiah 43:7).

If any of you wants to serve Me, then follow Me. Then you'll be where I am, ready to serve at a moment's notice. The Father will honor and reward anyone who serves Me (John 12:26 MSG).

God has built and equipped us for service to Him. To name a few, we have been adopted by Him and given the power to become sons of God; He has given us good and perfect gifts; we have been given delegated power and authority over demonic forces. He has placed treasures in our earthen vessel, and as a result of the treasures within, we are loaded with ideas, concepts, inventions, wisdom, and multiple gifts. In our inner man is untapped power and authority waiting to be released.

No matter how small the task, we each have been given an assignment to give God glory. Pharaoh's daughter was created to draw Moses out of the river. Jael was created to bring victory to Israel by driving a nail into the temples of Sisera. An unknown Egyptian was created to give direction to David so that he could pursue and recover all the Amalekites had taken from him. The widow Anna was created to serve God with fasting and prayers night and day. Vashti was created to make room for Esther. Judas, the son of perdition, was created to betray Jesus.

For the kingdom of heaven is as a man traveling into a far country who called his own servants, and delivered unto them his goods. And unto one he gave five talents to another two, and to another one; to every man according to his several ability, and straightway took his journey (Matthew 25:14-15).

The servant with five talents doubled what he was given; the servant who had received two talents doubled his also; the servant who received one talent buried his in the earth. The Lord said well done to the first two, but he told the last man that he was slothful. Proverbs 18:19 says, *"He also that is slothful in his work is brother to him that is a great waster;"* Ecclesiastes 10:18 says, *"Laziness leads to a sagging roof; idleness leads to a leaky house."*

Be determined to be on the move and always in transition. The enemy wants you to be stagnant; he wants to wear your mind down and render you weak. He bombards your mind with thoughts to produce fear and anxiety, so that he can remove your ability to manifest the will of God for your life. If your mind is weary, you will lose vision for your future. Allow the Lord to re-order your confidence in this hour over those little things that have captured and gnawed away at your strength and your productivity. Tell the devil you have an expected end, and it is documented in heaven.

When God trusts you with an assignment in the earth, your assignment must become an obsession. You must be diligent and faithful to the assignment. The greater the assignment, the more you must submit to God for direction and instruction. The greater the anointing that accompanies the assignment implies more knee (prayer) time. Humility is what you must present to the Lord: *For thus says the High and Lofty One who inhabits eternity, whose name is Holy: "I dwell in the high and holy place, with him who has a contrite and humble spirit"* (Isaiah 57:15).

The anointing requires a higher standard by which one must live their lives. When someone has been given much, much will be required in return. Your fruit must remain, so be diligent in praying and being committed to the work assigned to your hands. And remember this important fact, you cannot be about God's business if you are a man pleaser. The apostle Paul said, *"If I yet pleased men I should not be the servant of Christ."* People will attempt to persuade you to be out of the timing and will of God for your life. If you become anxious, the devil will step in and push you out prematurely, causing you to experience failure. Those who are trying to push you before time were not there to hear what God spoke in your ears. Stay with the time of God for every season.

You were created for His glory, not your glory. He has a purpose for everything He does. His timing for you is perfect. Perhaps the people God intends to bless you have not been properly aligned, or the Lord has not completed the process in you that is necessary for you to be all He has created you to be. Be determined to complete your assignment and finish your course. You were created to endure until the end. Everything negative that crosses your path will inevitably work together for your good. *For our momentary, light distress [this passing trouble] is producing for us an eternal weight of glory [a fullness] beyond all measure [surpassing all comparisons, a transcendent splendor and an endless blessedness]* (2 Corinthians 4:17 AMP).

Chapter 5

Rise Up, Come Up, Stay Up

Arise [from spiritual depression to a new life], shine [be radiant with the glory and brilliance of the Lord]; for your light has come, and the glory and brilliance of the Lord has risen upon you (Isaiah 60:1 AMP).

Circumstances can sometimes cause you to feel like saying, "I don't want to hear another prophecy or another sermon." Situations that happen in life may at times cause you to say or think, enough is enough, I give up, I cannot take it. Or, there may be times when you would rather do anything other than pray or read the Word because your prayers have not been answered yet. Or you may think that God is not listening, and you may think that you need to make things happen for yourself because God is too slow in His response or actions regarding your situation.

Life can literally be so rough that you just might begin to doubt that you ever heard from God, or that those words you wrote in your journal were words from your thoughts and not from the mind of Christ. Let us be real for a moment. Have you ever felt like depression can just come on in, take a seat, and escort you to your next level of misery? Yes, wonderfully anointed one, that can be the real deal experience at some point in your Christian journey. Our soulish emotions take over completely, and absolutely nothing spiritual is "kicking in" during that season.

But God!! It is a comfort to know that God trusts you to handle the test. He has confidence in your ability to rise up, come up, and stay up. He knows that despite what your flesh is screaming, the day will come when you will shake yourself from the bondage of depression, frustration, and negative circumstances and will begin to engage in the warfare necessary to bring you out victoriously.

I would like to be candid with you. I have experienced those times described above. It felt like a horde of demons had been assigned to me, and no matter how hard I fought, the fight became more intense. I did all the ABCs we are told to do, but seemingly nothing helped. It seemed as if God had abandoned me and I was fending for myself. I could not shake the oppression I was feeling. I read the Word; I decreed His promises; I fasted and prayed, but the battle continued to rage. One thing I knew for sure is that no matter what it looked like, the Word of

God is lethal. It is sharper than any two-edged sword; the Word is like a hammer and fire.

With the part of me, the spirit man that had been strengthened from the many years of reading and studying, I was able to rise up and put the armor of God on and fight my way out. May I add, the attack lasted for nine years in various forms, but I can now testify beyond a shadow of a doubt that I'm not the same woman I was when that battle began. I came out with a different mindset, a greater faith level, more wisdom from above, the spoils of the enemy and I am more skilled in spiritual warfare than ever. No matter what it looks like or feels like now, you will come forth as gold because you are more than a conqueror, and the weapon that was formed shall not prosper.

Death and life are in the power of the tongue, and they that love it shall eat the fruit thereof (Proverbs 18:21). Use your tongue to pray prayers that will cut through the earth's atmosphere, break the hemisphere, and get the job done. Boldly prophesy God's intent for your life. Strip, spoil, snatch, and seize with force what has been held up or stolen from you. Make up in your mind that you are a kingdom enforcer and that you will never be passive again. Be determined to rise up; take authority with a militant force and attitude.

When the enemy roars at you, remember the roar that is inside of you because of your relationship to the Lion of Judah. Rise up, come up and stay up.

Chapter 6

The Work of Holy Spirit

But, on the contrary, as the Scripture says, What eye has not seen, and ear has not heard and has not entered into the heart of man, [all that] God has prepared (made and keeps ready) for those who love Him [who hold Him in affectionate reverence, promptly obeying Him and gratefully recognizing the benefits He has bestowed]. Yet to us God has unveiled and revealed them by and through His Spirit, for the [Holy] Spirit searches diligently, exploring and examining everything, even sounding the profound and bottomless things of God [the divine counsels and things hidden and beyond man's scrutiny] (1 Corinthians 2:9-10 AMPC).

This is one of my favorite verses of Scripture because it lets us know that unlimited revelation and wisdom are available to the body of Christ. No wonder Paul prayed that the church at Ephesus would be given the spirit of wisdom and revelation in the knowledge of Him. With the combination of kingdom thinking and the spirit of wisdom and revelation, we can readily receive the deep and profound things Holy Spirit reveals.

On the throne of grace, our heavenly Father is discussing your future. Holy Spirit is attentive to all that is being said about you and your future because His plan is to reveal to you with accuracy and in complete detail what God has prepared just for you. Oh, you thought you were created to do menial tasks, or you thought the CEO of your company would recognize you for the hard work and numerous hours you worked, and that you would get the promotion that is long overdue. Or maybe you were hoping to be the supervisor over your department, the head teller at your bank, or that you are finally in a position to own that business you have always dreamed of. But, suddenly and continuously you begin to hear that still small voice in your heart, a voice that is speaking words of direction and instruction to your spirit that will change the course of life forever. What you are hearing is so astounding that you are literally gasping and wondering to yourself if, in fact, Holy Spirit has the right address. Yes, He has the right address.

You have spent years ministering to the Lord through prayer, worship, and fasting; you have been faithful to wait for your change to come; you have been steadfast; you have endured several tests that would have caused others to abandon the faith. You have loved the Lord with all your heart and mind. So today beloved is the day for the manifestation of those things that God has prepared just for you.

Now we have received, not the spirit of the world, but the Spirit who is from God, that we might know the things that have been freely given to us by God. These things we also speak.... (1 Corinthians 2:12-13)

Salvation and all the benefits of salvation are free. The fact that it is free may be the reason we have such difficulty receiving blessings from the Lord. We may think it takes total perfection on our part, or that we need to get all things right in order to be a recipient of those things that are freely given. The fact of the matter is all you and I have to do is say yes and amen to His will and thank Him.

The Bible tells us in the eleventh chapter of Mark verse 23 that if we do not doubt and if we believe then we shall have whatsoever we say. What we speak should be whatsoever Holy Spirit reveals. The Lord wants an agreement between heaven and earth; He wants Kairos to collide with Chronos so that His will can be done on earth according to His plan and architectural design in heaven. He told His disciples to pray thy kingdom come, thy will be done in earth as it is in heaven. The Lord wants those profound things that are being revealed from heaven to manifest in the earth realm expeditiously. This can be your reality if you are willing to repeat in the earth what Holy Spirit has spoken to your heart. Perhaps it may take a moment to comprehend all that is being downloaded into your spirit man. But remember, these are the things that your eyes have not seen, nor have your ears heard, nor have it entered into your heart, so of course what's been heard can be mind-blowing, and it may cause you to be awestruck at first. However, the sooner you begin to speak what He has said, the sooner the angels of God will go to work warring and strategizing to make those things which you spoke come to past. *Bless the Lord, ye His angels, that excel in strength, that do His commandments, hearkening unto the voice of His Word* (Psalm 103:20 KJV).

Speech is one of the most essential tools God has given to you. There is power in your tongue to give life or to cause death. The space we occupy is affected by the words you speak. You literally frame your world, create peace or chaos by your spoken word.

> ¹³*But the angel said to him, "Do not be afraid, Zacharias, for your prayer is heard; and your wife Elizabeth will bear you a son, and you shall call his name John..."*

¹⁸And Zacharias said to the angel, "How shall I know this? For I am an old man, and my wife is well advanced in years. ¹⁹And the angel answered and said to him, "I am Gabriel, who stands in the presence of God, and was sent to speak to you and bring you these glad tidings. ²⁰But behold, you will be mute and not able to speak until the day these things take place, because you did not believe my words which will be fulfilled in their own time" (Luke 1:13; 18-20).

Gabriel said your prayer has been heard as if Zacharias had prayed recently. However, remember, the man and his wife were both old and past childbearing age. The prayer was prayed long before the answer came, resulting in Zacharias' disbelief. After all, he no doubt prayed for a child when he was much younger. It would make sense in the natural to stop hoping for an answer to a prayer that "time and physical conditions" would cause to expire.

Prayer is mysterious. It is amazing and absolutely wonderful how the words spoken out of your mouth are seemingly suspended somewhere in the air, echoing throughout the atmosphere, waiting for one command, one wink, one nod, one thumb up from God to cause manifestation in the earth realm:

And we are confident that He hears us whenever we ask for anything that pleases Him. And since we know He hears us when we make our requests, we also know that He will give us what we ask for (1 John 5:14-15 NLT).

God is not human, that He should lie, not a human being, that He should change His mind. Does He speak and then not act? Does He promise and not fulfill? (Numbers 23:19 NIV).

Chapter 7

Take the Muzzle off Your Mouth
And Speak Forth Your Future

By faith we understand that the worlds [during the successive ages] were framed (fashioned, put in order, and equipped for their intended purposes) by the Word of God, so that what we see was not made out of things which are visible (Hebrews 11:3 AMPC).

God created the earth by merely speaking. With the understanding we have been created in His image and likeness, and have been given the mandate to subdue and take dominion, it should be obvious to you and me that our heavenly Father would expect us to frame our world by speaking His Word. *As He is, so are we in this world* (1 John 4:17). Mark 11:23 lets us know we can speak to the mountains and if our faith is engaged, we will see them removed.

The tongue in your mouth is full of power, force, and direction; when you speak, there is a force being released that will give direction to everything that is misaligned and will redirect everything that is assigned to you as your portion in it due season. As a result of being created in the image of God, the faith words spoken out of your mouth will frame and create your world, and cause it to be precisely what it was ordained to be before the foundation of the earth. Also, when you speak, your words are like sound waves in the spirit realm, like vibrations in the heavens. Your words are literally echoing. Your words are hovering like a plane waiting to land. The manifestation of your spoken word will not take place until God "nods His head," if you will, to indicate to His host that it's time for what you said in agreement with His will to happen. Therefore, it is crucial to be single-minded rather than double-minded.

Imagine yourself releasing words into the atmosphere that are full of faith and power, words that are decreeing who you are, while you are calling those things that be not as though they were because you believe what God has explicitly said to you regarding promises. Let us say you are excited and full of expectation, then suddenly a storm comes from nowhere—things today are not like they were on yesterday. Your language begins to change. Instead of decreeing, declaring, and speaking words of faith and allowing the power within to be released to change the course of the unexpected storm, you find yourself speaking negativity and words of doubt. Now, what do you suppose has happened to those words that were echoing and vibrating in the atmosphere? What happened to the words that were hovering, awaiting their due season of manifestation? A temporary distraction that brought about negative speech has now caused the angels assigned to carry out the promises of God for your life to turn back from gathering your goods because you changed your speech. Instead of going after what God has ordained for you to have, the angels assigned to you must now deal with fighting off the enemy's response to your doubt filled words.

Mark 11:24 says, *"Therefore, I say to you, whatever things you ask when you pray, believe that you receive them, and you will have them."* You and I must purpose in our hearts to believe God no matter what we see in the natural. We live by faith, not by sight; we will not see the manifestation of what we said immediately. This is why spiritual vision and the spirit of wisdom and revelation are important. They allow you to see what God sees and say what God says without a doubt.

When you are praying, especially praying in tongues, you are praying mysteries while at the same time, God is downloading His will into your spirit man. Holy Spirit is simultaneously revealing those profound things that you could have never thought of independent of God's thoughts. Once your spirit has received those profound mysteries, Holy Spirit expects you to speak what you heard and cause those things to manifest in the earth. Your words spoken in faith and in agreement with Holy Spirit will not fail to cause you to see everything you believe God for. Holy Spirit will inform you of God's plan and will continue to give you updated revelation concerning the mind of God as is relative to you. Once you hear the plan of God for you, your family, your business, or your ministry, you should begin taking dominion by speaking, decreeing, and declaring with confidence and boldness what Holy Spirit has told you. God said "His Word will not return to Him void;" everything promised you will become your portion if you hold that thought(s) and do not waver.

God is not a respecter of persons; He said whosoever, and that means you and yes you as well. You have been endowed with authority by Holy Spirit to speak to road-blocks, obstacles, distractions, and deceptions to tell them what they must do, that they have no legal authority and they all must go. They must all depart, and they cannot return. The power of your speech is connected to the faith you carry in your heart, so refuse to allow toxins to occupy space in your heart. *I will give you a mouth, and such utterance and wisdom that all of your foes combined will be unable to stand against or refute* (Luke 21:15 AMPC). The Word of God is sharper than any two-edged sword. Once you release His Word from your mouth, all your foes—known and unknown—will have to come down. You will not have to lift a finger to defeat the enemy; it is merely a matter of releasing His Word from your mouth. *My tongue is the pen of a ready writer* (Psalm 45:1b). Beloved, be ready at a moment's notice to write the script and to go to the next chapter in your life because the power, force, dominion, and ability to cause things to manifest are in your mouth.

Birthing requires you to say it until you see it; not only that, but you should maintain an attitude of worship and praise. Regarding Abraham, the Bible says in Romans 4:20 (AMPC), *"No unbelief or distrust made him waver (doubtingly question) concerning the promise of God, but he grew strong and was empowered by faith as he gave praise and glory to God."* Abraham gave praise to God prior to the birth of Isaac because *"he was fully persuaded that what God had promised, He was able to perform."* Purpose in your heart that you will embrace the same mindset Abraham had. Believe, expect, and anticipate, knowing our God will do it.

The Power of Prayer

Prayer is the avenue God has given for us to communicate with Him and He with us. Let us not complicate it; you are His child. For that reason, He enjoys the time of fellowshipping with you. Among other things, prayer enables you to become familiar with the Lord, His ways, His wisdom, and His love for you. While you are in His presence, prayer makes it possible for you to receive an impartation of strength, wisdom, direction, and power. In the book of Luke 11, verse 1, one of Jesus' disciples asked Him to teach them how to pray. The Lord's response was *"When ye pray, say, our Father which art in heaven, hallowed be thy name. Thy kingdom come. Thy will be done, as in heaven, so in earth"* (Luke 11:2 KJV). The Lord wants you to be kingdom minded and kingdom operable because the spiritual world rules the natural world.

Heaven has already mapped the plans out for your life; so, you must pray according to your assignment (His will)—that which you were created to do while on this earth. When you pray, pray realizing that prayer provides a means by which the spiritual realm interacts with the earthly realm: *Things which are seen were not made of things which do appear* (Hebrews 11:3).

Hebrews 4:16 says, *"Let us therefore come boldly to the throne of grace, that we may obtain mercy and find grace to help in time of need."* The Greek word for boldly is "parresia." It means frankness and outspokenness. God wants you to tell Him without hesitation and fear what your needs are as well as your desires. He says come to the throne, the place of sovereign power and authority. Come to the place of grace, favor, peace, pleasure, joy, and liberality. Come to the place where gifts are distributed and prayers are answered. He invites you and me to come with boldness. What an invitation from the Father!

In this atmosphere of extended grace, the tendency to be anxious is removed. Philippians 4:6 tells us to *"Be careful for nothing; but in everything by prayer and supplication with thanksgiving let your requests be made known unto God."* The Greek word for careful is "merimnao." It means to be troubled, anxious, fretful, or to be worried about something. Careful also refers to a person who is concerned about his ability to deal with life's daily issues. If you will permit the Word of God to be the ruler of your heart and "hold that thought," transformation will take place and the ability to have the mind of Christ, to hold the thoughts and purposes of His heart, will be your reality. Having His mind and His thoughts enables you to pray according to His design for your life.

Go into your prayer closet for the express purpose of obtaining a fresh anointing. Expect to receive more strength, power, might, energy, and fervency. Ask the Lord to teach you how to use heaven's authority and resources effectively. Be resolute as you are in His presence that you will not leave His presence the way you came in, but that you will exit your prayer closet with boldness, courage, and a made-up mind to be everything you have been chosen to be. Let "Yes and Amen" be the words you exit your prayer closet with.

Chapter 8

Attending the School of Faith

*Now faith is the assurance (title deed, confirmation) of
things hoped for (divinely guaranteed), and the evidence
of things not seen [the conviction of their reality—faith
comprehends as fact what cannot be experienced by
the physical senses]. For by this [kind of] faith the men
of old gained [divine] approval* (Hebrews 11:1 AMP).

The Lord's existence is in heaven, a place that is invisible
to us and where every phenomenon is supernatural. The
key to accessing this realm is through faith, which is our
connector, if you will, to the kingdom of God. Faith is a
substance, an assurance that everything God said to us in
His Word, as a promise, as direction for us personally or
for our family, or as a command concerning our assignment will come to pass no matter how, when, or where.
When we fully embrace faith, it will remove all doubt,
unbelief, and stress. We were saved by faith and by faith

we believe as a child of God that when we transition from this life, we will go to heaven to be with Jesus.

What I would like to call the "School of Faith" is where you go when God has determined He wants much more from you than you are currently giving. The Bible says in Romans 1:17b, *"The just shall live by faith."* However, when you attend "The School of Faith," there is seemingly more that is required. It is called being full of faith or having great faith.

Many people throughout the Bible displayed this level of faith. For example, Stephen in Acts, chapter 7, was full of faith. While being stoned, he was calling upon God and saying *Lord Jesus receive my spirit*; then Stephen said *lay not this sin to their charge.* Or consider the centurion in Matthew, chapter 8. He came to Jesus on behalf of his servant to ask that Jesus speak a word and heal him. Because of his great faith, Jesus healed his servant at that moment. Daniel, who after he was cast into the den of lions, came forth saying, *"My God sent His angel and shut the lions' mouths so that they have not hurt me"* (Daniel 6:22). Let us not forget Hananiah, Mishael, and Azariah, the three men who were thrown into a burning fiery furnace because they refused to worship an image:

They said, *"Our God whom we serve is able to deliver us from the burning fiery furnace, and He will deliver us from your hand, O king. But if not, be it known to you, O king, that we do not serve your gods, nor will we worship the gold image which you have set up"* (Daniel 3:17-18).

Here we are today in the millennium; some of us have more material things than we have ever had in our lives. Our sanctuaries are filled with thousands of attendees. The preached Word of God is easily accessible via the world wide web, Christian broadcasting, iPads, notebooks, and smartphones; yet the body of Christ has dwindling faith, is weak, fearful, and unfruitful. The focus is on non-essential things and material things rather than the things of the kingdom. So, we may wonder why all the struggles, test, and trials that obviously are lasting a lot longer than perhaps in previous years. We may be wondering, *Why haven't I come out of this thing yet?* Could it be it is because God is determined to have you and me live by faith? We are created in His image; therefore, we are built to live in the dimension of the supernatural—body, soul, and spirit. Faith should be dominant.

I must be candid when I talk about faith because I have just come out of a very, very long faith test. To be frank with you, I did not enjoy the test, nor did I score 100 percent in every area that I was tested in. The "School of Faith" offers advanced studies. You do not register to attend; you are just expected to be there on the day of roll call. I have had many, many test and trials throughout my life, so I thought I was a woman of great faith. I have believed God for some major stuff on many occasions, for many years. However, when the last faith test lasted nine years, I realized I was nowhere near having great faith.

While I was waiting for what God had promised to become a reality, I found that the enemy and his posse had turned up the intensity of the battle. My faith was tossed around like a ship in the water. It took me to the depths, brought me up for air, and then another giant wave came and took me to places where it was impossible (so I thought) for me to swim in. I thought I was going to drown in the waves of stress. I felt like God asked Satan the question, "Have you considered my servant Saundra." There were times when it seemed as if I could literally feel the hordes of demons that had been assigned to me by hell itself.

The fight to pass the test was real and intense. I did all the things we are supposed to do—prayed, fasted, decreed, declared, spiritual warfare, read the Word of God daily, and found my "lifeline" Scriptures. I had to hold on to every message I had preached, the promises He had made to me over the years, and every prophetic word that was written in my journals while holding on tightly to my God who seemingly had excused Himself from my situation. It took all I had to hold on to the truth. My faith was on the line.

But can I tell you I did not graduate from the "School of Faith" until I began to bring my head out of the situation? When I say to bring my head out of the situation, I am speaking of my thoughts that I forgot to hold on to. I had the manuscript for this book on my computer and in my heart for years, but I could not finish it until I had learned everything God wanted me to learn while in the "School of Faith." Holding on to the thoughts of actually seeing and experiencing all that God had promised me was not easy during that time. Throughout those years, I said, "I quit;" "God, what do you want from me;" "I'm going to sleep, wake me when it's over;" and the like. Well, do you think anything I said outside of what God had given me to say moved Him or caused heaven to be open over me? Not at all. If it had not been for some key people in my life, I would have been out for the count.

I think a valuable lesson concerning our belief in what God said is for us humans to avoid leaning to our own understanding at all cost. When God speaks to us, He speaks as if everything is done. He told the Israelites, *"I am the Lord your God, who brought you forth out of the land of Egypt, to give you the land of Canaan and to be your God"* (Leviticus 25:38). He did not mention that the land was inhabited by people who had no intention of giving it up without a fight. He failed to mention that the cities were heavily fortified and there were giants in the land. So, we skip happily along with limited information, thoroughly convinced that what God said is about to pounce on us. The tendency, at least for me, had been to calculate the time of manifestation, based on my perception of when I think I am ready and worthy to receive what has been promised because of all I have had to endure and was currently enduring. So, the clock began to tick in my head. When I felt it was the "now time," "the Kairos moment," and nothing showed up, boy was I perplexed, to put it mildly. No doubt, in between the promise and the place of provision, some significant storms and obstacles will try to block you from realizing the manifestation of God's promise, not to mention the devil's attempt to wear you out. So, I had to begin re-focusing in order to gain more wisdom about the ways and whys of God in order not to lose ground.

When the Bible says "the just live by faith," you had better believe it means what it says. Faith is not about quoting Scriptures as a ritual; living by faith involves action on your part. Faith without works is dead; it has no value to God. The Lord requires faith that is absolute—a faith that does not consider the present circumstances. God wants a faith that will cause you to see it as He sees it and say it as He says it. You and I are supposed to echo what was spoken to our spirit man by Holy Spirit without vacillating. Faith is the essential breeding ground for your visions and dreams to become a reality.

When challenges come, *"fight the good fight of faith"* (1 Timothy 6:12) during the wait. Remind God of His promises, posture yourself in prayer continually, and continue to believe that what He said shall come to past. The Israelites received according to their faith. They spoke fear, unbelief, and doubt and became recipients of their spoken words. Joshua and Caleb said to them, *"Do not rebel against the Lord"* (Numbers 14:9). Decreeing and declaring the promise(s) God made to you "does not an immediate manifestation make." You must be persistent in your declaration (whether it takes one day, one year, or many years). Be resolute and determined not to be moved by your current circumstances. To everything, there is a season. In your season called "due," what God promised you will become a reality. Faith, obedience, and your continued persistent agreement with the spoken promises are the keys to your receiving tangibly everything God promised you. I guarantee it will not be a moment too late: *For the vision is yet for an appointed time; but at the end it shall speak, and it will not lie; though it tarries; wait for it; because it will surely come, it will not tarry* (Habakkuk 2:3).

During my faith test, God wanted a broken alabaster box from me. He wanted me to display the kind of faith that would literally move mountains (enough of quoting the Scripture). He wanted the kind of faith that would cause devils to tremble. He wanted me to be so filled with faith that there was no room for unbelief. He wanted my yes to come from a deeper place in my spirit, and He was not letting up until He got what He was going after. Well, beloved, I graduated from the "School of Faith" (for a season at least and probably with a C-). However, on the other side of the thing called faith, I can honestly say it was worth it all.

I am not the same person I was in previous years. As a result of my personality type, I have always felt one does not need to hassle over the same problem over and over, praying about the same issue over and over. I believed that if God gave you the answer, just expect Him to do it; "Wait on Him," and do not continue asking people to pray for you about the same thing week after week after week. After going through for nine years, I am of a different opinion. I have a lot more compassion for people and am more relatable. I have been touched with the feelings of their infirmities. I also now know in my "knower" that I have attended the "School of Faith." By faith, I am now more equipped to do what I was created to do in this earth.

Chapter 9

The Stronghold of Hope

Return to the stronghold [of security and prosperity], you prisoners of hope; even today do I declare that I will restore double your former prosperity to you (Zechariah 9:12 AMPC).

Now to Him who is able to do exceedingly abundantly above all that we ask or think, according to the power that works in us (Ephesians 3:20).

When we lose hope, we lose faith, for faith is the substance of things hoped for. Our hope is received from the Lord; therefore, we must lean on Him and depend on Him for strength and guidance when the feeling of hopelessness tries to rear its head. In Zechariah 9:12, we are encouraged to return to the fortified place of hope and become a captive prisoner, so much so that we are literally bound to and attached to expectation. Upon our return to hope, we surrender to its fortification because we know as long as we are in that state, what we long for will become a reality. This time, we will not allow doubt, unbelief, and fear to creep in. No, we have had enough of that. We have returned to a holding place designed and protected by God. This is the one time we will eagerly say to our Lord, "Put the chains of truth and prosperity around my hands and feet and hold me tightly in the stronghold of hope."

Can you imagine having a mind that has been so transformed that it has yielded to the thought of being a prisoner who is always holding onto the thought of expectation with excitement because you now know that what you have been longing for will not tarry? Can you imagine that suddenly you have more than enough? Imagine that Ephesians 3:20 has come alive in your life, and you are experiencing the good life. Can you see yourself in your future, living in a wealthy place, and having full access to the valley of fruitfulness, the place of perpetual blessings? Imagine yourself being locked up in hope and going from strength to strength, peace to peace, joy to more joy, favor to more favor:

For the Lord God is a sun and shield, the Lord will give grace and glory; no good thing will He withhold from those who walk uprightly. O Lord of hosts, blessed is the man that trusts in thee (Psalm 84:11-12).

As a prisoner of hope, God promises you double restoration. I am sure a few of you have experienced some battles along the way. During those battles, you lost some stuff, perhaps it was a while ago, and you have forgotten about some of the stuff you lost. However, in the meantime, God has kept a record of all that has transpired in our lives. He remembers what you and I have forgotten. Some of what is coming your way in the form of a double portion is God's way of saying here are your spoils that have been accumulating over your years of faithfulness while you were enduring tribulations. God has numerous means of restoring what has been lost. He never ceases to amaze me. He will go ahead of us and cause mountains to become plains. He strategically puts people in place and causes them to seemingly bump into you at the right season for His purposes in your life.

In the book of Ruth, chapter one, Naomi had no idea that God was mindful of her in ways far beyond her ability to ask or think. She believed she was too old for anything new and different to happen in her life. Naomi had become bitter and wanted to be called Mara (bitter) because she thought God had dealt her a bad hand. She saw herself as being empty because of the loss of her husband and sons. But God had a plan in mind, and it started with Ruth, Naomi's daughter-in-law.

It is always to your advantage to allow God to connect you with people who can be instrumental in helping you reach your destiny. If not, you will find yourself connected to an Orpah, one who declines and is stiff-necked. Despite Naomi's discouraging words to her daughters-in-law, Ruth and Orpah, Ruth chose to ignore the obvious and trust in Naomi's God. Ruth said to Naomi, *"Don't ask me to leave you and turn back. Wherever you go, I will go; wherever you live, I will live. Your people will be my people, and your God will be my God"* (Ruth 1:16 NLT).

As a result of Ruth's faith and faithfulness to Naomi, she met and married Boaz, her kinsman redeemer, who happened to be a wealthy man. Ruth became the owner of the same land where she once hoped to obtain leftovers. The Bible says the Lord gave Ruth conception, and she had a son whose name was Obed; the father of Jesse, the father of David. As for Naomi, Ruth 4:14 says, *"Then the women said to Naomi, "Blessed be the Lord, who has not left you this day without a close relative; and may his name be famous in Israel!* Solomon wrote in Ecclesiastes 7:8, *"The end of a thing is better than the beginning."* Do not lose hope in your future. Hold that thought of becoming all God has promised you. Remain a prisoner of hope. Expect and anticipate experiencing the abundant life: *I will return her vineyards to her and transform the valley of trouble into a gateway of hope* (Hosea 2:15).

Chapter 10

Hold on To Your Vision

Where there is no vision [no redemptive revelation of God], the people perish (Proverbs 29:18 AMPC).

Where there is no revelation, the people cast off restraint; but the one who keeps the law is blessed (Proverbs 29:18 WEB).

The work of God provides vision and guidance. You will find that people will run amuck without vision and direction. Vision is provided to us by God for you and me to become familiar with His plans for your life. Vision also sustains you while you are nowhere trying to go somewhere.

10Now Jacob went out from Beersheba and went toward Haran. 11So he came to a certain place and stayed there all night because the sun had set. And he took one of the stones of that place and put it at his head, and he lay down in that place to sleep. ¹²Then he dreamed, and behold, a ladder was set up on the earth, and its top reached to heaven; and there the angels of God were ascending and descending on it. ¹³And behold, the Lord stood above it and said: "I am the Lord God of Abraham your Father and the God of Isaac; the land on which you lie I will give to you and your descendants. ¹⁴Also your descendants shall be as the dust of the earth; you shall spread abroad to the west and the east, to the north and the south; and in you and in your seed all the families of the earth shall be blessed. ¹⁵Behold, I am with you and will keep you wherever you go and will bring you back to this land; for I will not leave you until I have done what I have spoken to you" (Genesis 28:10-15).

For the next 21 years, Jacob had to hold on to the thought that he would one day own the land he had slept on, and that his descendants would be as numerous as the specks of dust on the earth. He would come to find out that the thought that would carry him through those years was that the Lord said, *"I will be with you and protect you wherever you go, and I will bring you back to this land."* Little did he know that he would have to work for his uncle for twenty-one years. He worked seven years to marry the woman he loved only to end up with her older sister Leah. Then, for Jacob to marry the intended bride, Rachael, he had to work another seven years. Laban made him build up his own flock from the worst of the bunch, and also he changed his wages ten times.

You know, when God gives you a promise, He omits the test and trials one has to experience before seeing the end of the thing. God gives us vision as an encouragement to hold on to the hope of receiving what has been promised. As I have held on to the vision God has given me, Romans, chapter four, has been a lifeline for me over the years. The Bible says of Abraham, *"When everything was hopeless, Abraham believed anyway, deciding to live not by what he saw he couldn't do but on what God said He would do"* (Romans 4:18 MSG).

Have you ever felt like giving up or like telling God, just give me the crumbs and forget giving me the whole loaf? The pressure of holding on the vision can be intense at times. But remember all things are beautiful in its time. There are specific times and seasons for everything concerning your life. Our Lord is not dependent upon clocks and calendars. In the kingdom of God, time is not of the essence. He works all things out in accordance with His will and His purpose. He is the beginning and the end, He lives in all "time"—past, present, and future. He has already seen you "there," while you see yourself "here."

His thoughts toward you are good, and He will make sure you arrive at the place of expectation on "time."

While you are waiting for the manifestation of the vision to become a reality, keep your mind free of toxins and debris: *Be sober, be vigilant; because your adversary the devil, walks about as a roaring lion, seeking whom he may devour (seize upon, destroy, and consume)* (1 Peter 5:8). Satan is cunning, shrewd, influencing, and determined. He is a wise strategist, he plans and systemically executes his assaults. Spiritual warfare is waged in the mind because it is the place where thinking, reasoning, understanding, and remembering takes place. Negative and positive imprints are embedded in your mind.

Failure to cast down negative experiences from your mind will result in the enemies' fiery darts penetrating those toxic areas and causing the debris to spread to the mind's healthy areas where truth resides. This will leave you without strength to prevail with the belt of truth mentioned in Ephesians, chapter six, as part of the armor of God. Satan knows if he can leave an indelible imprint on your mind, he can use your past experiences and mistakes to make you feel guilty with the hopes of preventing you from experiencing the vision God gave you for your future. The enemy fights you and me hard in an attempt to wear us out, take our vision, and cause us to be dull of hearing: *This vision is a witness pointing to what's coming. It aches for the coming, it can hardly wait! And it doesn't lie. If it seems slow in coming, wait. It's on its way. It will come right on time* (Habakkuk 2:3 MSG).

The Grasshopper Mentality

> *And we were in our own sight as grasshoppers, and so we were in their sight* (Numbers 13:33b).

The grasshopper mentality produces negative thoughts that end in sure defeat. It causes low self-esteem and self-image that will cause you to question your worth, qualification, confidence, and God's ability to perform what He promised. It causes a nomadic mindset—aimless roaming, wandering from place to place without a plan and without vision. First Corinthians 2:14 (KJV) says, *"The natural man receiveth not the things of the Spirit of God: for they are foolishness unto him; neither can he know them, because they are spiritually discerned."* The carnal mind operates by reasoning and has no spiritual insight:

> *He hath blinded their eyes (meaning there is no vision or imagination), and hardened their heart (the heart is not pliable); that they should not see with their eyes, nor understand with their heart, and be converted (changed), and I should heal them* (John 12:40 KJV).

The devil and his crew's desire for you and me is for us to be as vagabonds, a people with no hope, always begging, always in a constant state of poverty, desolate, and in want for our entire life.

This book of the law shall not depart out of thy mouth; but thou shalt meditate therein day and night, that thou mayest observe to do according to all that is written therein; for then thou shalt make thy way prosperous, and then thou shalt have good success (Joshua 1:8 KJV).

Your destiny is based on the truth you know. You have been given a sound mind, a mind that is saved, delivered, and protected and secure from outside influences. So, gird up the loins of your mind, guard it with all diligence, keep your mind fortified with the Word of God. Make a vow to yourself that you will no longer view yourself as unimportant and defeated and that you will move from struggling to reigning in life. Say to yourself, "I refuse to allow the enemy of my soul to cause my mind to be weak; I am persuaded in my mind that I am destined to be successful and that I will reach my destiny."

Isaiah 26:3-4 (KJV) says, *"Thou wilt keep him in perfect peace, whose mind is stayed on thee: because he trusteth in thee. Trust ye in the Lord for ever: for in the Lord Jehovah is everlasting strength."* The word peace in this verse means shalom (health, happiness, and wellbeing) in the Hebrew language. By dwelling in His presence, you will find yourself experiencing clarity of thoughts that will free you up to receive a constant flow of wisdom, revelation, and knowledge from Him. Continual communication will result in shalom being your portion.

Chapter 11

The Appointed Time

To everything there is a season, and a time to every purpose under the heaven (Ecclesiastes 3:1).

Our times, opportunities, and open and closed doors are in the hand of the Lord. Patience is paramount while waiting on the season that is appointed by God for your life because you and I are limited when it comes to having knowledge and wisdom of God. Going ahead of God may very well result in disasters and catastrophes that will demand full play requiring you to remain in the situation you created until it has played out. Jude 25 says He is the only wise God. The Lord Jesus Christ has a fullness of time for everything and a scheduled appointment for all things to come to pass. In His timing, you will find that He does the unusual, the unique, and the extraordinary. He chooses people, tools, and avenues that you would most likely overlook.

God is more concerned with your integrity, steadfastness, faithfulness, and commitment to His kingdom's way of doing things than supplying everything you want at a rapid pace or giving you a quick fix type answer and solution. The Lord told Habakkuk, *"These things I plan won't happen right away. Slowly, steadily, surely, the time approaches when the vision will be fulfilled. If it seems slow, do not despair, for these things will surely come to pass. Just be patient. They will not be overdue a single day."* (2:3 TLB).

A man's mind plans his way, but the Lord directs his steps and makes them sure (Proverbs 16:9). While you are waiting for your "due" season, practice being comfortable where God has you; enjoy the moment. Spend time delighting yourself in Him. Avoid becoming a self-appointed assistant to God. Avoid impulsive moves; it can be tempting to move out ahead of God and do your own thing, but that very thing could cause the promise to be extremely delayed or worse yet God could repent of the promise He made you (see 1 Samuel 15:35).

The War in The Wait

I had fainted, unless I had believed to see the goodness of the Lord in the land of the living (Psalm 27:13).

Holding on to the thought while waiting for God's divine purpose, will, and promises to come to past in your life can be a challenging process. I am sure you have heard some people mention the struggle that takes place from the time the promise is revealed until there is an actual manifestation.

> *6Wherefore say unto the children of Israel, I am the Lord, and I will bring you out from under the burdens of the Egyptians, and I will rid you out of their bondage, and I will redeem you with a stretched out arm, and with great judgments: 7And I will take you to Me for a people, and I will be to you a God: and ye shall know that I am the Lord your God, which bringeth you out from under the burdens of the Egyptians. 8And I will bring you into the land, concerning the which I did swear to give it to Abraham, Isaac, and to Jacob; and I will give it you for a heritage: I am the Lord (Exodus 6:6-8 KJV).*

As far back as I can remember, I have always loved the Lord. My parents did not have to make me attend church; I just did. I always went to church alone (without my parents), because my mother owned and operated a corner grocery store that was opened every Sunday without fail; therefore, she was unable to accompany me to the services. My mother was a no-nonsense kind of woman. What she said she meant. She came from the "real old school," which meant I was not allowed to attend parties, date, etc. When I turned 18, I was "out" of the house. I wanted to see what I had been missing all those years. Yet still while trying to embark upon my new-found freedom, no matter what I did on Saturday night, I had to attend church on Sunday. At that time, I served God based on the truth I knew and understood. My thoughts were *Surely, He doesn't mind the clubbing and the unmentionables I was doing*. After all, I had been denied experiencing the world's fun all my life. So, for whatever reason, God allowed me to "do my thing" until I was forty-one years of age and when things were finally going well for me.

A girlfriend and I had decided to go to a club after work (a very boring evening by the way). While we were having our drinks and sitting there, I heard the Lord say to me, "If I return tonight, you won't return with me." I thought to myself, *I'm not going to hell because I'm sitting in a boring club.* That was a defining moment for me and the beginning of a very serious walk with God. Everything came to a halt. I made as many small changes in my life as I could. For instance, I stopped going out to clubs and drinking. However, the Lord had to intervene in the other worldly things I was participating in, and intervene He did.

Shortly after the club intervention, the Lord would instruct me to go to the Valley Forge Park on my lunch hour. There He spoke to me about His divine plan for the rest of my life. He told me how He would bless me, and there would be no lack in my life and so forth. What He did not tell me was that He expected me to quit my job, which I did. He failed to mention that I would lose my home and become homeless. He did not tell me I would lose my automobile and have to ride the bus and trolley (which I had not ridden in over 20 years at that time. He did not tell me I would have absolutely no money and that I would have to totally depend on Him to touch people's hearts to provide for my daughter and me.

I learned quickly how to depend on Holy Spirit to guide me through the rough terrain. When the troubles came, I had to keep believing. I was determined to hold on to the promises by not exalting my circumstances above His Word. Holding on to the thought required steadfastness, being fixed, having unshakable faith and a love for God, that caused me to realize that whatever hardship I was experiencing was a light thing. Oh yes, it took some days of not feeling like holding on. Through this process, there were days of saying, "I'll take the crumbs, instead of the promised loaf if you'll end this test now." There were days when I thought I must have missed God because surely all He told me He would do should have happened by now. There were periods of intense warfare when the devil's lies would echo in my mind, and I had to fight to hold onto the truth I knew and believed. I learned in this process how to decree His promises to me. I had to say it until I saw it. I also learned how to take the sword of the Spirit and wield it against the enemy to annihilate every obstacle he put in my path.

In this process of waiting, I found in my arsenal the weapon of praise. I learned to create an atmosphere for my Father to inhabit while at the same time confusing the enemy with my praise. The devil loves to see us defeated while waiting on God's promises to become a reality in the earth. The Bible says in 2 Chronicles 20 that as Israel began to sing and praise, the Lord set ambushes against the enemy. Praise and worship confuse the enemy and provides an atmosphere for victory in spiritual warfare.

It was during that long process of waiting for His promises to become a reality that He prepared me to serve Him. I had always prided myself in my ability to "make things happen." I would only call on the Lord if I were unable to help myself. I was always told I had to take one step for Him to take two; my one step became long strides. While I was waiting for the promise to become a reality, the thing that kept me going was all that He had spoken to me while in Valley Forge Park. I had no idea that it would take many, many years to see, touch, and feel all the things that God had promised me. But note, I said "things." Matthew 6:33 says, *"But seek ye first the kingdom of God, and His righteousness, and all these things shall be added unto you."* My back was up against a wall. I could not depend on myself; I had to rely totally on God for everything, and I could only do that by seeking His kingdom through prayer and fasting and by being totally obedient to Him and finally by becoming childlike in my approach to the kingdom of God.

While I was waiting for God to give me "things," He was downloading wisdom, revelation, and knowledge. He was endowing me with a supernatural strength to endure, stand, and be steadfast. While I was waiting on things, He downloaded a "liquid love" into the spirit of a woman who had not known real love. He caused me to love Him with my entire being, and suddenly the things I was waiting for became irrelevant.

I have learned that the waiting process can be considered a form of grace and mercy in that if I had been given everything He had promised during my early forties, I would not have the wisdom necessary to hold on to the things He wanted to give me because the mall was my drug of choice. My every extra spare dollar went to the support of the King of Prussia Mall. I had no respect for the money I was to steward over until I had no money to steward over. I had to learn how to master money as opposed to money mastering me.

Chapter 12

The Fight That Follows Illumination

But call to remembrance the former days, in which, after ye were illuminated, ye endured a great fight of afflictions; ³³*Partly, whilst ye were made a gazing stock both by reproaches and afflictions; and partly, whilst ye became companions of them that were so used.* ³⁴*For ye had compassion of me in my bonds, and took joyfully the spoiling of your goods, knowing in yourselves that ye have in heaven a better and an enduring substance.* ³⁵*Cast not away therefore your confidence, which hath great recompence of reward* (Hebrews 10:32-35).

You can be sure that if you respond by faith to a promise received from the Lord, negative thoughts will invade your mind. The enemy of your soul will do anything and everything possible to try to persuade you not to do what God has called you to do. When you first received the dream, vision, or word from the Lord concerning His promise to you, there is unavoidable excitement.

However, the longer it takes for the dream to come to pass, the more the burning in your heart depreciates. If you are not careful to stand on His promise, the hope of a manifestation ends up being oblivious. When you let go of your hope, dream, vision, and promise, it is equal to letting go of your destiny and your calling. This is where you fight to hold that thought: *Let us hold fast (embrace it tightly, possess it, take control of it, dominate it) the profession of our faith without wavering, for He is faithful that promised* (Hebrews 10:23).

There is a season for everything. God trusts you with advanced information by allowing you to see where you are going while you are still in the midst of turmoil, hurt, pain, disappointments, doubt, fears, and you can continue to fill in the blanks. I believe He allows us to see the future so that we can embrace the mindset as Abraham, *"who against hope believed in hope, that he might become the father of many nations; according to that which was spoken......."* You will have many opportunities to be full of doubt throughout the process of "becoming."

I must be candid and say the fight for illumination can at times make you feel like saying forget it. I'll keep the room and forget the house. I'll continue flipping burgers because the struggle to finish the course can be overwhelming. There may be times when you feel like your prayers are not being answered, and God has left the room. Oh yes, the thoughts and the desire to throw in the towel are real.

Satan's mission is to wear your mind out, cause you to question truth, and render you hopeless. But, thank God for Holy Spirit and for the fact that He is in you and He is great inside of you. The thing is this: Hell must be thoroughly convinced of the fact that you realize you have authority and that you know you have the victory. Yes, you may feel defeated for a brief moment, but remember, weeping endures for a night, but joy comes in the morning. Beloved, when your morning comes, you will eat at the table that has been prepared for you in the face of your enemies.

No question about it, you will have to fight a few battles before you see a manifestation of the promise. However, during the fight, you will find appearing on the scene a supernatural uprising in your spirit that will cause you to be combative and resolute. You will be able to be fully persuaded as Abraham was, that what God has promised, He is able to perform.

Chapter 13

It Is About That Time

For I know the thoughts that I think toward you, saith the Lord, thoughts of peace, and not of evil, to give you an expected end (Jeremiah 29:11 KJV).

While you were holding your thought, the Lord was right there with you, building and strengthening your inner man, causing you to be stronger, to be more faithful, giving you keener vision, teaching you how to pursue Him. He was there all the time teaching you how to fight the good fight while placing a desire for the more of Him. Your expected end is upon you and the waiting period is just about over. A manifestation of what you have been praying for, believing for, hoping for, and trusting God for is quickly becoming your reality. Look with anticipation toward seeing His manifested glory like never before and believe that the season of abounding grace and the shield surrounding favor is about to overtake your life.

In this season of birthing, live on purpose in the atmosphere of expectation. Suddenly and at a moment's notice, your circumstances can change because God is able to immediately restore, realign, and make whole all things. I believe you are in your time of Kairos—when the immediate is about to overtake you: *So let us seize and hold fast and retain without wavering the hope we cherish and confess and our acknowledgment of it, for He who promised is reliable [sure] and faithful to His Word* (Hebrews 10:23 AMPC).

It took one day for Joseph to go from prison to the position of governor. In one day, Ruth moved from the position of gleaning the leftovers to ownership of the field. In one day, the Israelites moved from the position of slavery to the position of freedom that included seizing the spoils of the enemy. Have faith in the Lord's ability to cause the unexpected to happen for you. After all, you are in covenant with God: *The secret of the Lord is with them that fear Him, and He will show them His covenant and reveal to them its deep inner meaning* (Psalm 25:14).

In One Day

In the book of Esther, we find a young lady who had experienced the loss of both of her parents. She was taken from her hometown of Jerusalem into captivity in Persia.

Hebrews 10:35-36 says,

"So do not throw away this confident trust in the Lord. Remember the great reward it brings you. Patient endurance is what you need now so that you will continue to do God's will. Then you will receive all that He has promised."

The KJV says in verse 35, *"Cast not away, therefore, your confidence, which hath great recompense of reward."* God has a unique way of reimbursing us for all losses due to "wars" of any kind, be it the loss of time because of being a part of the world or restoration because of what the thief took.

The only relative mentioned in the book of Esther was her cousin Mordecai, a man who had taken on the role as her father, a man whom Esther respected, and a man to whom she was obedient. In Esther, chapter 1, we find that king Ahasuerus had a feast for many days. When the "heart of the king was merry with wine," or to put it another way, once he was drunk, he commanded those who served him to bring Vashti the queen before the people to show off her beauty, but she refused to come. In my opinion, Vashti was a woman of class and purpose, a woman who refused to be on display in front of a bunch of drunken men. However, God was in the background preparing for a "one day turn around experience" for another woman.

The Bible lets us know that promotion comes from God; He opens and closes doors, and He decides when your season is up or due. So, despite Vashti's integrity, her season was up: *If it pleases the king, let a royal decree go out from him, and let it be recorded in the laws of the Persians and the Medes, so that it will not be altered, that Vashti shall come no more before King Ahasuerus; and let the king give her royal position to another who is better than she* (Esther 1:19). The king issued the decree and Vashti's reign as queen was up.

In one day, Esther's script was about to flip. Just when you begin to think *I give up*, God will nod His head or point His finger in your direction and cause a suddenly and immediately to show up in your life. Your Kairos (now) moment has shown up unexpectedly. Your now time, your season, the promises, and the vision you have been holding on to have appeared without warning.

Now that Vashti was out of the picture, and the king was sober and realizing he was without his wife, he began to search for a particular kind of woman (see Esther 2:2-4). Listen, beloved, you were fearfully and wonderfully made for a divine purpose; no matter your build or your nationality, God did not miss it when He created you. In this case, the chosen woman happened to be a beautiful virgin. Esther was created to look the way she looked because she needed to have entrance into the king's palace in order to be chosen. Although she was chosen by the palace maidens, she was not ready to stand before the king because she had to go through the process of preparation which required twelve months of purification.

There you are, on the other side of the door of opportunity, but wait! You still have the dust from your past. You are still thinking like a slave. You have to be processed. You have to be prepared. You are getting ready to transition from Salvation Army, Goodwill, thrift store, J. C. Penney, and Target clothing to Bloomingdales, Nordstrom, Neiman Marcus, Armani, Gucci, Louis Vuitton, Marc Jacobs, Oscar de la Renta, and Versace attire. You are about to put "rocks" on your finger and a Rolex on your wrist. You are about to go from walking or riding public transportation to being chauffeured in a Bentley limo. You must be prepared for the suddenly this change is presenting. So, allow God to carry you through the unchartered paths, through the valleys, and up the mountains to prepare you for what you were created to do.

The king's heart is in the hand of the Lord, like the rivers of water; He turns it wherever He wishes (Proverbs 21:1). After Esther had gone through the preparation period, the hand of God and the grace of God was on her: *And the king loved Esther above ALL the women, and she obtained grace and favor in his sight more than all the virgins; so that he set the royal crown upon her head, and made her queen instead of Vashti* (Esther 2:17). When God has a divine plan for your life, nothing stops Him. He will turn a person's heart and superimpose His will for your life on their heart without them realizing "God did that."

Get ready, for your one day to become your reality. I know you have been waiting and waiting, but believe me, you are on the absolute brink of a one-day turnaround. Go to the zone of expectation and anticipation and remain there until your day of grace and favor shows up.

Chapter 14

Be Determined to Recover It All

So David recovered all that the Amalekites had carried away, and David rescued his two wives. And nothing of theirs was lacking, either small or great, sons or daughters, spoil or anything which they had taken from them. David recovered all (1 Samuel 30:18-19).

During your times of struggle, endurance, and patience, the Lord was THERE, building your inner man, causing you to be stronger, more faithful, teaching you how to have a keener vision, causing you to seek Him. He was also teaching you how to fight the good fight of faith, while at the same time placing inside of you a desire for the more of Him. The Lord was encouraging you so that you would hold on to your vision, dreams, hope, and faith in Him. And to recover all the enemy stole from you, He was teaching your hands to war.

The enemy is familiar with the fact that the Lord loves His children and that He trains and teaches us how to war and recover our spoil. The enemy of our soul also knows that our training consists of gaining of more strength, wisdom, and power along with the fact that you and I are given strategic facts on how to be victorious in every battle. So, while we are in The Lord's "Strategic Kingdom Training Camp," the devil is doing everything possible to break our focus, steal our joy, disrupt our peace, weaken our minds, steal our health and finances, touch our loved ones, destroy good friendships and marriages, etc. That being said, we must refer to Ephesians 6:17: *And take the helmet of salvation, and the sword of the Spirit, which is the Word of God.* The Greek word for "word" is hray-mah. We know this word as Rhema, which means something that is spoken clearly, vividly, or in certain definite terms.

A Rhema word is a specific word that Holy Spirit quickens in our hearts and minds at a specific time and for a special purpose. The Rhema word repels the attacks of the enemy and is supernaturally empowered by God to enable us to withstand the mental, emotional, spiritual, and physical attacks of the enemy: *I will give you a mouth and such utterance and wisdom that all of your foes combined will be unable to stand against or refute* (Luke 21:15). The power in your mouth is direction, dominion, and force.

You must engage your words when attempting to recover everything that has been taken from you.

"Pursue and Recover It All"

The question becomes, how bad do you want it. If you are determined to gather all the spoils due you, you must be a kingdom enforcer: *Whatever you bind on earth will be bound in heaven; whatever you loose on earth will be loosed in heaven.* Command the enemy to take his hands off your stuff. Take immediate authority over him. You must muster up all your strength and pursue and recover it all. Matthew 11:12 says, *"And from the days of John the Baptist until now the kingdom of heaven suffereth violence, and the violent take it by force."* Taking by force means to strip, spoil, snatch, and seize with force.

Do not be passive, but be aggressive, take authority, be hostile, attack first, be combative and militant as you regain your territory: *Behold, I give unto you power (authority, strength, jurisdiction) to tread on serpents and scorpions, and over all the power (force, ability, strength, mighty work) of the enemy, and nothing shall by any means hurt you* (Luke 10:19). Call on your back up. God has appointed His angels to protect and rescue you from spiritual and physical harm: *The angel of the Lord encampeth (pitch a tent, abode) round about them that fear Him, and delivereth them.* (Psalm 34:7 KJV).

Guard Your Heart

Above everything else, guard your heart; for it is the source of life's consequences (Proverbs 4:23 CJB).

The heart in the above Scripture is referring to a person's intellect, emotions, and will. The heart is where you are to hide and keep God's Word. It is the "filter" for your thoughts; from it, you can choose good or evil thoughts or deeds. The heart is the place where belief is birthed. The heart is central to your life because your will and the Lord's will are supposed to be in sync at all times. Therefore, the heart must be kept and guarded constantly. There must be a twenty-four-hour, seven days a week watch because the enemy wants to cause a "traffic jam" in your emotions. The devil's desire is for you to listen to his lies, to become double-minded, unsettled, and shaken, while the Lord wants you to remain focused, steadfast, and fixed on His Word.

You must make a quality decision to follow after and pursue God and His ways with all your heart. Have a determination to remain nestled in the secret place of the Most High, keep your ears pressed to His mouth, while always listening for instructions and the reiteration of His promises. No doubt you will find our Lord encouraging you and reminding you that He is mindful of you and all that concerns you.

A heart that has been guarded and protected from negative intrusions is a heart that will be flooded with life. That life will in turn flow throughout your being to cause an overflow of the flow, resulting in your environment and circumstances taking a turn for the better. As a result of guarding your heart against lies and deception, you will attract new friends (with like mindsets), and everything under your sphere of influence will begin to take on a new look because you have allowed life and truth to flow from your heart.

Persevere Until Something Happens

The word persevere means to be steadfast, persistent, resolute, determined and endurance. When you decided to persevere, you are saying I refuse to surrender in the face of difficulty, no matter how tough things are and no matter how great the failures have been, I will never quit. Proverbs 24:10 MSG) says, *"If you fall to pieces in a crisis, there wasn't much to you in the first place."* The Amplified Bible (Classic Edition) says, *"If you faint in the day of adversity, your strength is small."* The day of adversity is the day of trouble, difficulties, misfortune, and confusion. Adversity is the test of your strength.

For a just man falleth seven times, and riseth up again (Proverbs 24:16 KJV). Listen, you can determine in your mind that you have God's grace which will cause you to arise with the "bounce back anointing." If you will just be determined to hold on to the promises of God, His promises will sustain and strengthen you, because you are thoroughly convinced that the weapon formed simply will not prosper. Every situation has a life span. If you magnify the situation, you will prolong its life span. However, if you endure by fighting the good fight of faith, you will shorten the life span of the situation.

They shall not be ashamed that wait for Me (Isaiah 49:23). As you wait in God's presence, you are exchanging your weakness for His strength. His strength will revive you amid your weakness. In His presence, you will obtain the ability to rise above your difficulties and soar like an eagle. In His presence, you will receive the ability to run spiritually without tiring and to walk forward without fainting, because the power of God will begin to flow through your very being. You will emerge with power, might, and authority. Pursue, chase, and overtake until what you have heard from God becomes your reality in the earth realm. Keep plowing until that hard ground of failure and limitation breaks up completely. Before you know it, you will be enjoying every promise God has made to you because YOU decided to Persevere Until Something Happens.

Be Stirred Up to Finish

Land on your knees and bring it all forth. Call things that are not as though they were. Declare your vision with a new boldness. Write down and plan to work the new strategies. Receive fresh oil. Operate from the position of having received new strength:

> *For verily I say unto you, that whosoever shall say unto this mountain, be thou removed, and be thou cast into the sea; and shall not doubt in his heart, but shall believe that those things which he saith shall come to pass; he shall have whatsoever he saith* (Mark 11:23 KJV).

You, yes YOU, can talk to your mountains of fear, doubt, unbelief, envy, hurt, anger, bitterness, past limitations, poverty, low self-esteem, unforgiveness, and jealousy and tell it to be moved NOW! YOU can move on to your wealthy place of favor, rest, perpetual abundance, peace, and joy. YOU can enjoy the perpetual flow of His anointing which provides fresh ideas, motivation, strength, and expectation. YOU were created to endure until the end. Everything that crosses your path must be placed in the note called "ALL THINGS ARE WORKING TOGETHER FOR MY GOOD."

Always remember you have bragging rights without the need to apologize. STIR yourself up; be bold and courageous. Stir up your power to imagine and to conceive what you have imagined. Know that you qualify to have and to hold onto every thought God has given you.

About the Author

Apostle Saundra L. Hagans is founder and pastor of Covenant House of God Church. She is a committed and dynamic vessel of God. In 1993, having been filled with a burning vision to reach the lost in a dying world, she birthed Covenant House of God Church with fifteen people in her living room.

There is a tangible anointing upon her ministry that set captives free of every demonic stronghold. Salvation, healing, and deliverance permeate every aspect of her ministry, and her inspirational preaching and teaching stir a revival and hunger for God in the hearts of believers everywhere. Her gifts of Holy Spirit are evident in the power of her preaching as she exhorts and encourages individuals to move from glory to glory and from deep to deep.

To inquire about Apostle Saundra Hagans speaking, ministering, or doing book signings and discussions at your church or event, you may contact her at:

saundra.hagans@gmail.com
or
(215) 329-5258

For more information about this book, please contact:

Kingdom Living Publishing
P.O. Box 660
Accokeek, MD 20607

publish@kingdomlivingbooks.com

(301) 292-9010

Or visit www.kingdomlivingbooks.com